HELLOOOOOOO, READER! WELCOME TO THIS MAGICAL BOOK THAT WILL CHANGE YOUR LIFE!

SUPER MAGIC WAND

THE WORDS (EXPERTLY WRITTEN) AND THE PICTURES (NOT SO WELL DRAWN) ARE BY ME

FRANÇOIZE

YOU GOT IT! I'M YOUR NEW AWESOME HAPPINESS COACH!

BIG SHOW-OFF!

WALKER BOOKS FOR YOUNG READERS
AN IMPRINT OF BLOOMSBURY
NEW YORK   LONDON   NEW DELHI   SYDNEY

TO START WITH...

HERE'S A LITTLE DIAGRAM TO SHOW HOW MUCH EVERYBODY ON THE PLANET WANTS TO BE HAPPY!

I WANT TO BE HAPPY!

AND ME!

GLOBAL SALES OF THIS AMAZING BOOK

GLOBAL SALES OF CHOCOLATE BARS

GLOBAL SALES OF CHEWING GUM

BEST SELLER

#1

#2

#3

EVEN WHEN THINGS DON'T LOOK GREAT...

EVERYBODY CAN LEARN WHAT TRUE HAPPINESS IS!

STUPID WORM

PHEW! WELL THAT'S GOOD NEWS! EVEN I CAN LEARN, THEN!

ALL LIVING CREATURES RECEIVE
THE MAGICAL GIFT OF LIFE, BUT YOU ARE
EXTRA LUCKY BECAUSE YOU ARE:

100% HUMAN

AND SO YOU GET ALL THE SPECIAL
PRIVILEGES RESERVED FOR HUMANS,

LIKE, FOR EXAMPLE:

· · · · · · · · · · · ·

WEARING NAIL POLISH

I AM RICH

GETTING POCKET MONEY

BEFORE   AFTER

CHOOSING YOUR HAIRSTYLE

BURP

PFFFT

STUFFING YOURSELF WITH PEANUT BUTTER

THINKING ABOUT YOUR FUTURE JOB

LION TAMER

ARE YOU SURE?

USE YOUR LITTLE BRAIN TO THINK ABOUT ALL THE OTHER ADVANTAGES!

HERE ARE A FEW EXAMPLES OF NON-HUMAN LIVING THINGS, WHO ARE A LOT LESS LUCKY THAN YOU:

NO FRIENDS ON FACEBOOK

WILL NEVER KNOW WHAT LOVE IS

Oh, woe is me! What a miserable life!

CAN'T SEE A PSYCHIATRIST WHEN THINGS AREN'T GOING WELL

HAS NEVER BEEN AWAY ON VACATION IN ITS LIFE

HAS NEVER SEEN THE SEA

CAN'T WEAR A COAT
TO KEEP WARM IN WINTER

* (TRANSLATION: I'M ABSOLUTELY FROZEN!)
(GET ME A TICKET TO HAWAII, QUICK!)

*

BRRRRRRRR!
BRRRRRRRR!

DOESN'T KNOW HOW
TO PUT UP A TENT

ONLY HAS ONE PAIR
OF UNDERPANTS, AND
THEY'RE MADE OF FUR

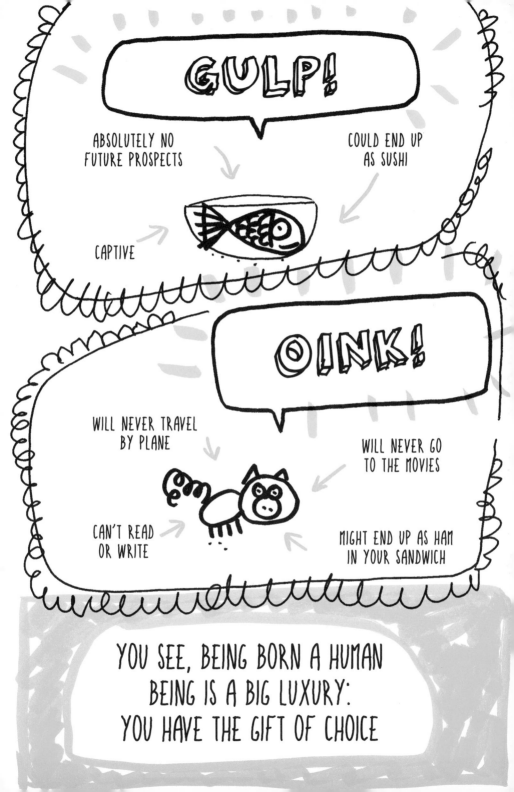

GOOD NEWS: YOU CONTROL YOUR LIFE!

IT'S UP TO YOU TO THINK CAREFULLY AND FILL IT WITH EVERYTHING YOU LOVE TO MAKE IT EXTRAORDINARY

UGH! I DON'T WANT THAT! YOU MUST BE JOKING!

EXAMPLE 1

A TINY SHRIVELED-UP LIFE, FULL OF SAD AND BORING THINGS

YUMMY! I WANT THAT!

EXAMPLE 2

A LIFE FULL OF HAPPINESS, LAUGHTER, AND FUN

THE BAD NEWS:
HAPPINESS DOESN'T JUST
FALL OUT OF THE SKY.
(WHAT A SHAME!)

24-HOUR HAPPINESS DELIVERY SERVICE

PACKAGES FULL
OF GOODIES
AND DELIGHT

A HUMAN BEING SQUASHED
BY TOO MUCH HAPPINESS
(YES, IT DOES HAPPEN)

I WANT
SOME!

ME
TOO!

MONEY-BACK GUARANTEE IF YOU'RE NOT HAPPY!
IS THIS MAD WOMAN EVER GOING TO STOP YELLING?
HMM... SOUNDS LIKE A CON TO ME. YOU'D BE BETTER OFF JUST READING THIS BOOK! IT HAS SOME GREAT IDEAS IN IT TO MAKE YOU HAPPY
WORM GLOWING WITH INTELLIGENCE

I'M AFRAID BEING HAPPY IS HARD WORK, BUT IT'S DEFINITELY WORTH THE EFFORT!

TAKE YOUR OATH HERE:

 1

PLACE YOUR LEFT HAND ON YOUR HEART

 2

CLOSE YOUR EYES (READ ALL THE INSTRUCTIONS FIRST)

JUST SAY YOUR OATH IN YOUR TINY HEAD!

THIS OATH IS TOTALLY USELESS! WHAT ABOUT PEOPLE WHO DON'T HAVE ANY HANDS?

MAKE SURE YOU ALWAYS REALIZE WHEN YOU ARE HAPPY!

VERY IMPORTANT!

PHILOSOPHICAL BUTTERFLY →

REMEMBER! THE MORE YOU'RE AWARE OF YOUR HAPPINESS, THE GREATER IT IS!

'CAUSE HOW SILLY WOULD IT BE TO BE HAPPY AND NOT EVEN REALIZE IT!

HAPPINESS MAKES YOU FEEL LIKE YOU CAN FLY, FLY, FLY...

YAHOO! CHEEP! CHEEP!

WOO-HOO! CHIRP! CHIRP!

CLOUD LAYER

DARLING, WHO ARE THOSE TWO SHOW-OFFS WEARING ONLY UNDERPANTS WHO THINK THEY'RE BIRDS?

THEY'RE SUPER-HAPPY HUMANS WHO FLOAT PAST FROM TIME TO TIME...

EARTH

HAPPINESS CAN MAKE YOU SMILE LIKE AN IDIOT

A WHAT YOU LOOK LIKE MOST OF THE TIME

B AFTER AN AWESOME PIECE OF NEWS

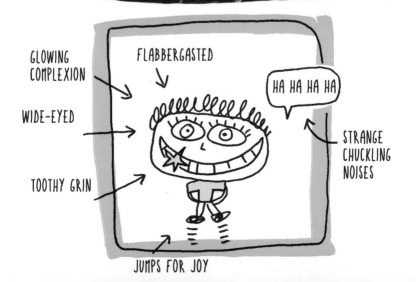

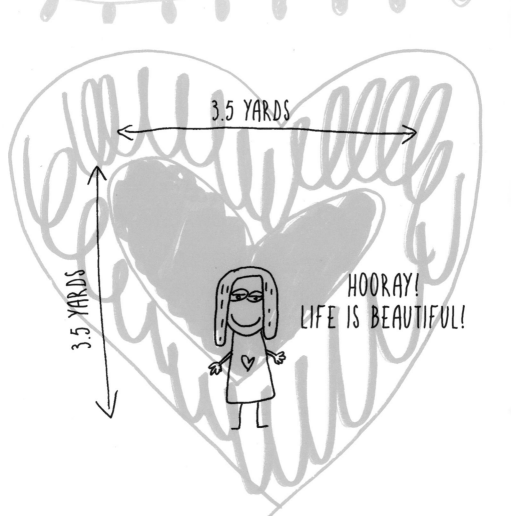

YOU MAY EVEN FEEL LIKE YOUR HEART IS GETTING BIGGER THAN YOU!

3.5 YARDS

3.5 YARDS

HOORAY! LIFE IS BEAUTIFUL!

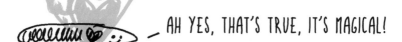 — AH YES, THAT'S TRUE, IT'S MAGICAL!

HAPPINESS MAKES YOU GLOW

IT FILLS YOU WITH AMAZING ENERGY

HAPPINESS IS CONTAGIOUS: IF YOU'RE HAPPY, YOU MAKE THE PEOPLE WHO LOVE YOU HAPPY!

YOUR GRANDPARENTS

YOUR REAL FRIENDS

YOUR DAD

HOORAY!

YOUR MUM

HOORAY!

YOU, HAPPY

THIS BOOK IS SERIOUSLY COOL!

YOUR DOG

YOUR WORST ENEMY

YOUR GOLDFISH

YOUR BEST FRIEND

THIS IS A PRINTING ERROR

ALL THIS HAPPINESS CAN'T LAST; I'M SURE SOMETHING AWFUL IS GOING TO HAPPEN

EXCEPT THOSE WHO ARE REALLY JEALOUS: HMPH!

HAPPINESS IS LIKE A MAGNET: IT ATTRACTS LOADS OF PEOPLE WHO WANT TO SHARE IT WITH YOU

AND THAT'S GREAT, BECAUSE BEING HAPPY BY YOURSELF IS A COMPLETE WASTE OF TIME

HAPPINESS IS INFINITE: THERE'S ALWAYS ENOUGH FOR EVERYONE...

PROOF

WHAT'S THE DIFFERENCE BETWEEN A HUGE CAKE AND HAPPINESS?

A

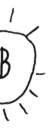

B

HAPPINESS

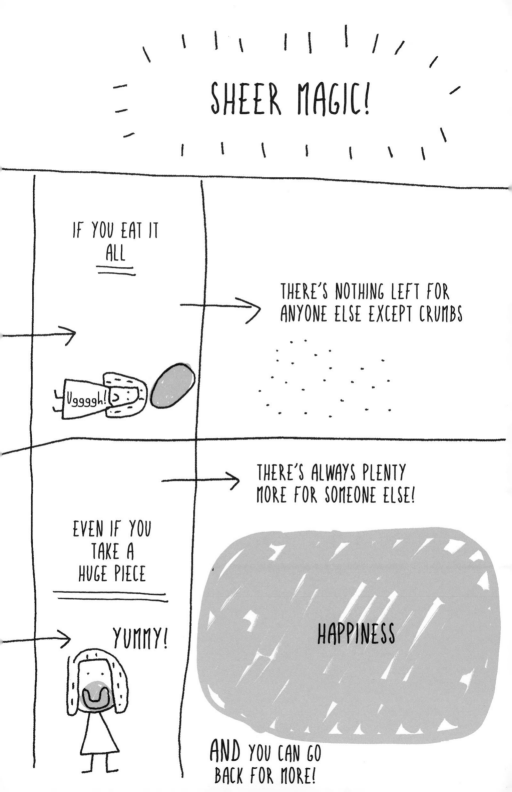

EVEN WHEN YOU THINK HAPPINESS SOMETIMES PLAYS HIDE-AND-SEEK WITH YOU... IT'S NEVER FAR AWAY

DON'T WORRY!

pile of yucky things that sometimes happen in life

HAPPINESS HIDDEN AWAY, BUT YOU'LL FIND IT AGAIN VERY SOON

WHAT'S THIS BIG BLACK THING? HELP, I CAN'T SEE HAPPINESS ANYMORE!

AND THEN YOU CAN BECOME GREAT FRIENDS!

QUIZ

FIND THE 2 UNHAPPY PEOPLE ON THIS PAGE WHO HAVEN'T BEEN LUCKY ENOUGH TO READ THIS AWESOME BOOK

TOO EASY! DOES SHE THINK YOU'RE AN IDIOT?

DRAW YOURSELF SWIMMING IN HAPPINESS!

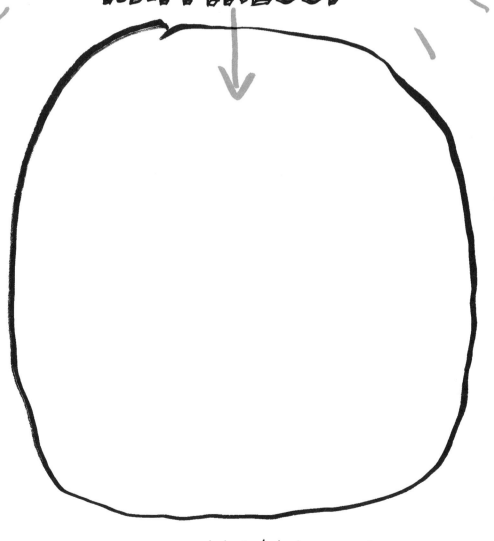

BE CAREFUL NOT TO DROWN!

EXTRA SPECIAL IMPORTANT ADVICE

WATCH OUT! THE RIGHT-HAND PAGE IS VERY SCARY!!!

HELLOOO, READER!
I'M YOUR LUCKY STAR;
LOOK AT ME EVERY TIME
YOU NEED SOME LUCK!

EXAMPLES

TO PASS A TEST THAT YOU HAVEN'T STUDIED FOR AT ALL	SO NOBODY WILL NOTICE YOU'VE DONE SOMETHING STUPID
TO IMPRESS THE GIRL OR BOY OF YOUR DREAMS AT A PARTY	SO YOU DON'T GET CAUGHT TELLING BIG, FAT LIES

DO YOU THINK THIS STAR REALLY HAS MAGICAL POWERS? OR IS IT A LOAD OF NONSENSE?

OF COURSE IT DOES! I LOOKED AT IT AND I HAD CAVIAR FOR SCHOOL LUNCH, I GOT 21 OUT OF 20 ON AN EXAM, AND THE BEST-LOOKING GUY IN THE WHOLE WORLD TOLD ME HE LOVES ME!

TURN OVER QUICKLY TO DISCOVER THE BASIC RULES OF BEING HAPPY!

→

RULE No. 1

SPREAD LOVE ALL AROUND

AMONG THE PEOPLE WHO SURROUND YOU

AND IN EVERYTHING YOU DO (YOUR HOMEWORK FOR EXAMPLE)

↑

ARE YOU CRAZY?

LOVE

LOVE

LOVE

LOVE

NUTS!

RULE No. 2

ALWAYS LOOK ON THE BRIGHT SIDE OF LIFE

LIKE HIM:

I MAY BE A WORM, BUT AT LEAST I DON'T
SPEND MEGA BUCKS ON NAIL POLISH, RINGS,
SNEAKERS, OR JEANS THAT'LL BE OUT OF
FASHION IN 3 DAYS' TIME.
GET IT?

RULE No. 3

ENCOURAGE FRIENDSHIPS

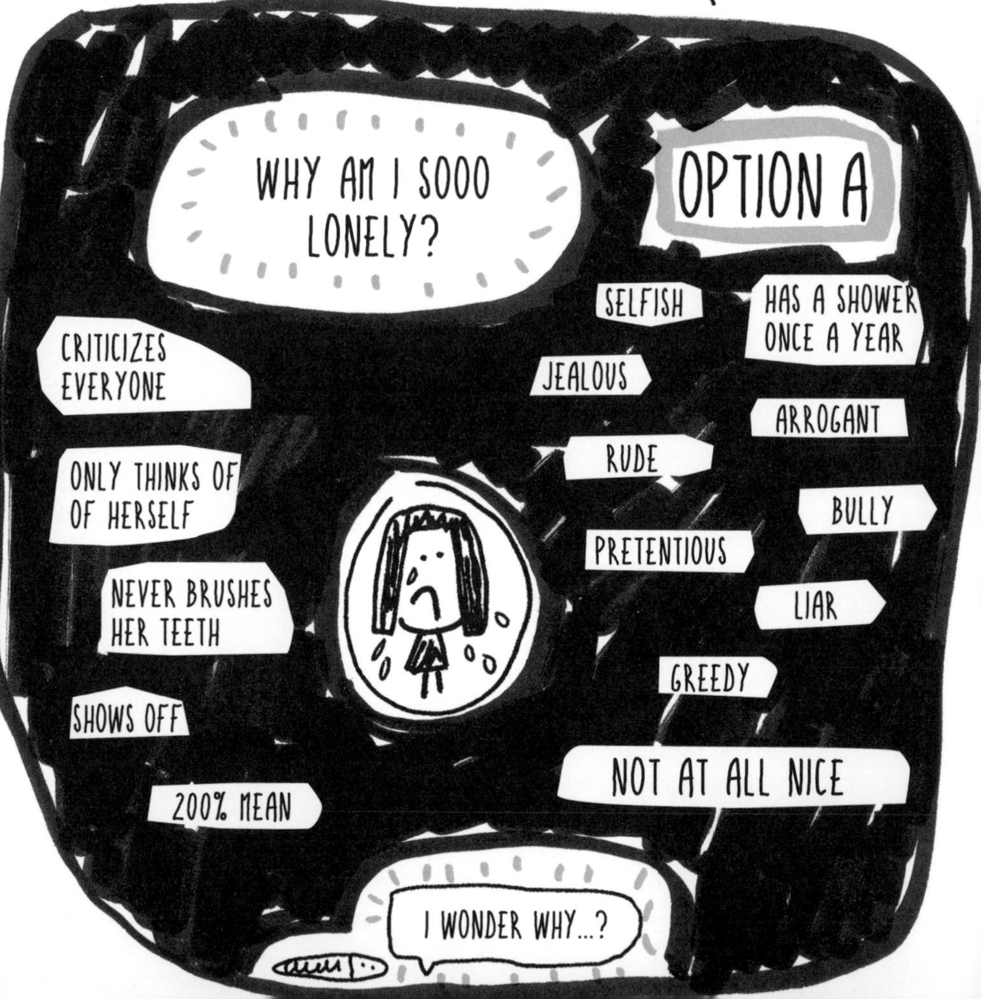

RULE No. 4

FREEDOM IS ESSENTIAL FOR HAPPINESS

1 EVEN IF YOU SOMETIMES *FEEL* LIKE YOU'RE IN PRISON...

NO YOU CAN'T GO LIVE WITH YOUR FRIENDS IN NEW YORK IN SEPTEMBER!!!! HA HA HA HA HA!

GRRRR RRRR!

HOME SWEET HOME

CRUEL, SARCASTIC LAUGH

YOUR MEAN, TORTUROUS PRISON GUARDS

KEY

YOUR DAILY RATION OF STEAMED ZUCCHINI

YOU

BALL AND CHAIN (OR WHAT IT FEELS LIKE ANY

AT LEAST YOU'RE FREE TO **THINK** WHAT YOU WANT

PLEASE LET THEM SUDDENLY COLLAPSE WITH INDIGESTION FROM EATING VEGGIES, SO I CAN LIVE MY LIFE HOW I WANT

GENIE AND LAMP

3 YOU CAN **SAY** WHAT YOU WANT (BUT CONSIDER THE CONSEQUENCES CAREFULLY)

YUCK!

STEAMED ZUCCHINI IS DISGUSSSSSTING! ARE YOU TRYING TO KILL ME?

4 AND IN A FEW YEAR'S TIME YOU'LL BE **COMPLETELY** FREE

YOUR DESTINY

I'M FREEEEEEEEEEEEEEEE! GOOD-BYE AND THANKS FOR <u>EVERYTHING</u>, YOU OLD FARTS! SEE YOU! I'LL BE BACK WITH MY DIRTY LAUNDRY!

A FAREWELL SPEECH THAT SHOWS YOUR PARENTS HOW GRATEFUL YOU ARE FOR THE HAPPY CHILDHOOD THEY GAVE YOU (I HOPE)

RULE No. 5

DOWN WITH VIOLENCE! PEACE RULES!

WATCH OUT! SPECIAL GUEST STAR!

RAYS OF LIGHT

LEVITATION

THE GREAT MAN OF PEACE HAS COME SPECIALLY FROM PEACELAND TO WRITE SOMETHING IN THIS BOOK

HEY BUTTERFLY, WHO'S THE BALD GUY WITH THE GIRL'S DRESS???

????

I'VE GOT NO IDEA!

100% FORBIDDEN!

HEY, FISH FACE! YOU'RE NOT MY FRIEND ANYMORE!
I'M GONNA THROW CAKE AT YOU, STEAL
YOUR HAMSTER, AND RUIN YOUR LIFE,
SO GO ON AND CALL YOUR MOM!

 GRRRR GRRRR

HELP!
MOOOM!

200% RECOMMENDED

GRRRR THIS IDIOT
IS REALLY ANNOYING!

ARGH!
WHAT A DOPE!

ALWAYS MAKE A HUGE EFFORT, EVEN
IF IT'S A STRUGGLE SOMETIMES!

A MIRACULOUS LITTLE RITUAL TO CARRY OUT EVERY SINGLE DAY

READ THE OPPOSITE PAGE IN THE MIRROR EACH MORNING BEFORE YOU BRUSH YOUR TEETH →

IN THE MORNING

OKAY, I'VE GOT MY FALSE TEETH, SOME TOOTHPASTE, A TOOTHBRUSH, AND A LITTLE MIRROR, SO I CAN TRY THIS LITTLE EXPERIMENT TOO...

HAVE AN AWESOMELY WONDERFUL DAY, DUDE!

AND HERE
ARE A
FEW HINTS
ON HOW
TO BE
EVEN
HAPPIER
==>

BELIEVE IN YOURSELF 100%

SUPER POWERS!

NO DOUBTS WHATSOEVER

YESSS, I CAN DO ANYTHING! WHERE THERE'S A WILL THERE'S A WAY!

HAVE CONFIDENCE IN YOURSELF

BUT NOT IN HIM

VERY FIERCE DOG

STOP THAT RIGHT THIS MINUTE! IT'S VERY HARMFUL TO HAPPINESS!

I'M SUPER GOOD-LOOKING, SUPER INTELLIGENT AND EXCEPTIONALLY GIFTED, BUT VERY MODEST. I'VE GOT A PERFECT BODY, I'M INCREDIBLY BRIGHT WITH A SENSE OF HUMOR TO DIE FOR... IN FACT, I'M JUST SOOO HAPPY TO BE ME!

UM, AREN'T YOU A BIT FULL OF YOURSELF, TOO?

BUT REMEMBER, THIS DOESN'T MEAN YOU DON'T HAVE ANY FAULTS AT ALL!

CHOOSE YOUR FRIENDS CAREFULLY!

B A REALLY BAD CHOICE:

YOU GET THE PICTURE, RIGHT?

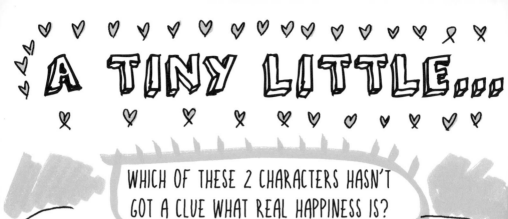

A TINY LITTLE...

WHICH OF THESE 2 CHARACTERS HASN'T GOT A CLUE WHAT <u>REAL HAPPINESS</u> IS?

WHEN I GROW UP I'M GOING TO MARRY A TALL, BLOND SUPERMODEL, EARN ZILLIONS, DRIVE A STRETCH LIMO, HAVE CAVIAR FOR BREAKFAST, BE ON TV, HAVE MY OWN PRIVATE JET AND YACHT, A MEGA-HUGE OFFICE WITH A THICK CARPET, AND BECOME BEST FRIENDS WITH THE PRESIDENT.

CANDIDATE 1

BE GENEROUS AND SHARE WITH YOUR FRIENDS!

RIDICULOUS EXAMPLE

WHO WANTS SOME HEADLICE IT'S FREE???

WANT A NICE LITTLE FLU BUG?

OR HOW ABOUT A SUPER DOSE OF CHICKEN POX?

ACHOO!

SO DO YOU WANT SOME, OR NOT?

INNOCENT PASSERBY

HOORAY! HOORAY! EVERYTHING IS FREE!

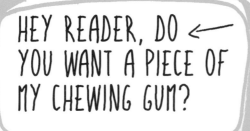

SCALE OF HAPPINESS

KEEP TRYING
DEPTHS OF DESPAIR
• STILL HASN'T UNDERSTOOD THE BASIC RULES ABOUT BEING HAPPY
• NEVER CONTENT
• PESSIMISTIC
• ALWAYS WHINING
• NEGATIVE
GRRRR! IT'S ALL BAAAAAAAD!
GET IT?

GET RID OF FEAR AND SHYNESS IN 4 EASY STAGES

STAGE NO. 1 → THINK OF SOMETHING YOU'D LOVE TO DO BUT ARE TOO SCARED

STAGE NO. 2 → REPEAT 2,500 TIMES IN FRONT OF A MIRROR:

EASY PEASY!
I CAN DO IT!
I REALLY CAN!
IT'S SOOOOOOO SIMPLE!

COOL, RELAXED ATTITUDE

WHISTLING

SMILE!

HANDS IN POCKETS

STAGE NO. 3 → CLOSE YOUR EYES AND IMAGINE YOU'RE A SUPERHERO!

100% EFFECTIVE
PEP TALK

I'M THE GUY WHO ISN'T SCARED OF ANYTHING! I'VE GOT SUPERHUMAN POWERS!!! NANANANANA!

STAGE NO. 4 → THEN... JUMP RIGHT IN WITH BOTH FEET!

EXAMPLE ON NEXT PAGE

← SEE PREVIOUS PAGE

GO FOR IT! GO ON! YOU'VE GOT NOTHING TO LOSE!

 ← SLOBBERY FAN

EXAMPLE: IN THE PLAYGROUND

YOU, TRANSFORMED INTO A
BLOCK OF PURE CONFIDENCE

TOTALLY-OUT-OF-YOUR-LEAGUE
MOST POPULAR GIRL IN SCHOOL

REACTION A

REACTION B

HELLO, GIRL I LIKE, HOW ABOUT COMING TO THE MOVIES WITH ME ON WEDNESDAY?

??

FASHIONISTA   GODDESS   INCREDIBLE

BEAMING
WITH PRIDE

AHHHH AT LAST HE'S MADE UP HIS MIND! I'VE BEEN WAITING FOR THIS PRECIOUS MOMENT SINCE NURSERY SCHOOL...

GODDESS PASSED OUT WITH PLEASURE

10:01 AM → POSSIBLE REACTION NO. 2

GREAT...

HOW DARE YOU SPEAK TO ME, YOU STUPID BOY!

BUT AT LEAST YOU WON'T HAVE ANY REGRETS!

STOP THINKING THAT THE GRASS IS ALWAYS GREENER...

THE WHATDOYOUCALLITS GO TO HAWAII EVERY WEEKEND, THEY'VE GOT 4 LIMOS, THEY HAVE FRIES WITH EVERY MEAL, THEY GO TO BED AT 3 AM AND WHEN THEY POOP IT SMELLS REALLY NICE!

JEALOUSY ACNE →

LUMP IN THROAT →

REALLY WANTS TO CRY ↗

IT'S SUCH A MESS AT OUR HOUSE

WE ALWAYS EAT ORGANIC FOOD

MOM AND DAD MAKE US LISTEN TO THE TALK SHOWS ON THE RADIO

CLOSE YOUR EYES AND THINK ABOUT EVERYTHING THAT'S REALLY GREAT IN YOUR LIFE!

IF YOU'RE A WORM...

1 NO DIRTY PANTS AND SOCKS TO PUT IN THE LAUNDRY BASKET

2 DON'T HAVE TO KISS BRISTLY OR SMELLY PEOPLE

3 DON'T HAVE TO WORK

4 WILL NEVER HAVE TO WEAR BRACES ON MY TEETH

5 AND THERE ARE LOADS MORE I'VE FORGOTTEN

WOO-HOO!
MY LIFE IS JUST HEAVEN!

DREAM PAGE

BE INQUISITIVE!
EXPLORE, DISCOVER, AND UNDERSTAND THE MYSTERIOUS, MAGICAL WORLD AROUND YOU...

FOR EXAMPLE: MODERN ART

MASTERPIECE FROM THE MUSEUM OF MODERN ART

OH REALLY? ARE YOU SURE IT ISN'T A PIECE OF DOG POOP?

SO IF I PAINT THE SAME THING, WILL I GET 300 MILLION DOLLARS?

DON'T LISTEN TO THE TERRIBLE SPOILSPORTS
(A VERY DANGEROUS SPECIES)

IT'S GOING TO SNOW

NO FUTURE

THE WORLD WILL DEFINITELY END ON DECEMBER 34TH!

UNLESS YOU GIVE ME ALL YOUR MONEY

GREEDY GURU

THIS BOOK IS SERIOUSLY STUPID! DO YOU REALLY FIND IT FUNNY?

I WANT TO BE A ROCK STAR!

OH, COME ON, ACTUALLY GET REAL! YOU'LL NEVER MAKE IT, SO WHY BOTHER TRYING!

YOU'LL END UP POOR, UNEDUCATED, OUT-OF-WORK, OVERWEIGHT, AND ABANDONED IN A STINKY DUMPSTER!

PHONY CLAIRVOYANT →

THE ANSWER

SUPER EARPLUGS©

THESE EARPLUGS WILL KEEP YOU FROM HEARING ALL THE WORDS THAT COULD SHATTER YOUR DREAMS

HE MUST TAKE ME FOR
A REAL NINCOMPOOP!!

DOES HE THINK HE'S
THE ONLY CHILD IN
THE WORLD?

I'M GOING TO GIVE HIM COAL;
THAT'S ALL HE DESERVES!!!

YET ANOTHER STUPID HUMAN
WHO HASN'T UNDERSTOOD THAT
HAVING MILLIONS OF USELESS
THINGS DOESN'T MAKE YOU HAPPY?

IT'S ENOUGH TO MAKE YOUR
CHRISTMAS TREE BREAK OUT IN HIVES!

P.S. AND IF YOU
DON'T GIVE ME
ABSOLUTELY
EVERYTHING ON THE
LIST, I'LL THROW
A TANTRUM!

WHAT'S MORE, ALL
THOSE PRESENTS POLLUTE
THE PLANET

SUPER-SMART TALKING CHRISTMAS TREE

DON'T TRY TO BE LIKE EVERYONE ELSE

IF YOU DO, LOOK AT WHAT MIGHT HAPPEN AS YOU COME OUT OF SCHOOL

LATEST FASHION HIGHLIGHTS

SUPERSTAR GLASSES

FAKE DIAMOND TONGUE PIERCING

"PEACE AND LOVE" FAKE FACIAL TATTOO

GOTHIC BIKER JACKET

LEATHER MINISKIRT

INSTEAD, DECIDE WHAT MAKES YOU REALLY HAPPY AND JUST DO IT!

WHY NOT MAKE A LIST OF THE
MOST INTELLIGENT ACTIVITIES
THAT MAKE YOU SUPER HAPPY!

I'VE GOT IT!
I LOVE WEARING COSTUMES!

AND SKATEBOARDING
ROCKS!

NOT TRUE! YOU BIG LIAR!

NEWLY STYLED HAIR →

← COACH POTATO

LAZYBONES →

← DISCO SHOES

HAWAI

ENJOY THE GREAT OUTDOORS!

SHORT GREEN MESSAGE

GO DIVING

OCTOPUS SEVERELY AFFECTED BY SEA POLLUTION

AMAZING TREASURE THAT CONTAINS ANSWERS TO ALL MATH EXAMS

LOOK AT THE SKY, THE STARS, AND CLOUD FORMATIONS

PRINCIPAL OF YOUR SCHOOL

JAR OF NUTELLA

TOO PRETTY

PFFFFTTT →

SO WHAT? IT'S ONLY NATURAL

HOLD ON NOW, THIS IS A CHILDREN'S BOOK, YOU KNOW!!!

DON'T SPEND YOUR LIFE
GLUED TO A SCREEN!

DON'T SPEND YOUR LIFE
GLUED TO A SCREEN!

DON'T SPEND YOUR LIFE
GLUED TO A SCREEN!

DON'T SPEND YOUR LIFE
GLUED TO A SCREEN!

YOU'LL TURN INTO A
MEGA-STUPID COUCH POTATO

I'VE REPEATED MYSELF TO GET MY
MESSAGE ACROSS, PLUS IT MEANS I DON'T HAVE
TO DRAW ANYTHING ON THIS PAGE! HA HA HA!

TRY TO BE WITH REAL PEOPLE IN THIS WONDERFUL REAL LIFE!

ADVANTAGES OF REAL PEOPLE

YOU CAN TOUCH THEM

KISS THEM

TICKLE THEM

HOLD THEIR HANDS

HUG THEM

KNOW IF THEY'RE COLD OR HOT

WHISPER SWEET NOTHINGS IN THEIR EARS

FEEL THEIR SKIN

STICK YOUR FINGER UP THEIR NOSE
PINCH THEIR BOTTOM

SMELL THEIR PERFUME

THE BEST THING: THEY'RE ALWAYS THERE, EVEN WHEN YOUR COMPUTER AND YOUR TV HAVE BROKEN DOWN!

REAL LIFE IS JUST TOO WONDERFUL!

A LITTLE AERIAL VIEW

SATELLITE VIEW OF THE EARTH

(A) BEFORE THIS BOOK WAS PUBLISHED

(B) AFTER THIS BOOK WAS PUBLISHED

THE NUMBER OF SUPER-MEGA-HAPPY CHILDREN IN THE WORLD

WOW!

AFTER THIS BOOK
WAS PUBLISHED

Ⓐ

BEFORE THIS BOOK
WAS PUBLISHED

HA HA HA, MY TUMMY HURTS FROM LAUGHING!

CALL AN AMBULANCE!

HA HA HA
HE HE HE HE
HO HO HO HO HO!

BUT PLEASE, NEVER LAUGH AT PEOPLE, IT'S REALLY NOT FUNNY

HEY, READER, HAVE YOU SEEN THAT GIRL'S FACE?
DO YOU THINK SHE'S THE SOLE SURVIVOR OF A NUCLEAR EXPLOSION?
OR OF A GLOBAL MEASLES EPIDEMIC?
OR MAYBE SHE'S BEEN ATTACKED BY CRUEL ALIENS
FROM OUTER SPACE!

TRY TO CHANGE THINGS FOR THE BETTER WHERE YOU CAN...

BEFORE → AFTER

EXACTLY BETWEEN THE 2 IS JUST PERFECT

HERE

YOU, SUPER LAZYBONES

YOU, WORKAHOLIC

YOU SEE, YOU CAN DO IT!

BUT ALSO ACCEPT THERE ARE THINGS YOU CAN'T CHANGE

MAKE SURE YOU'RE IN SHAPE ALL THE TIME

CASE NO. 1: YOU, UNFIT

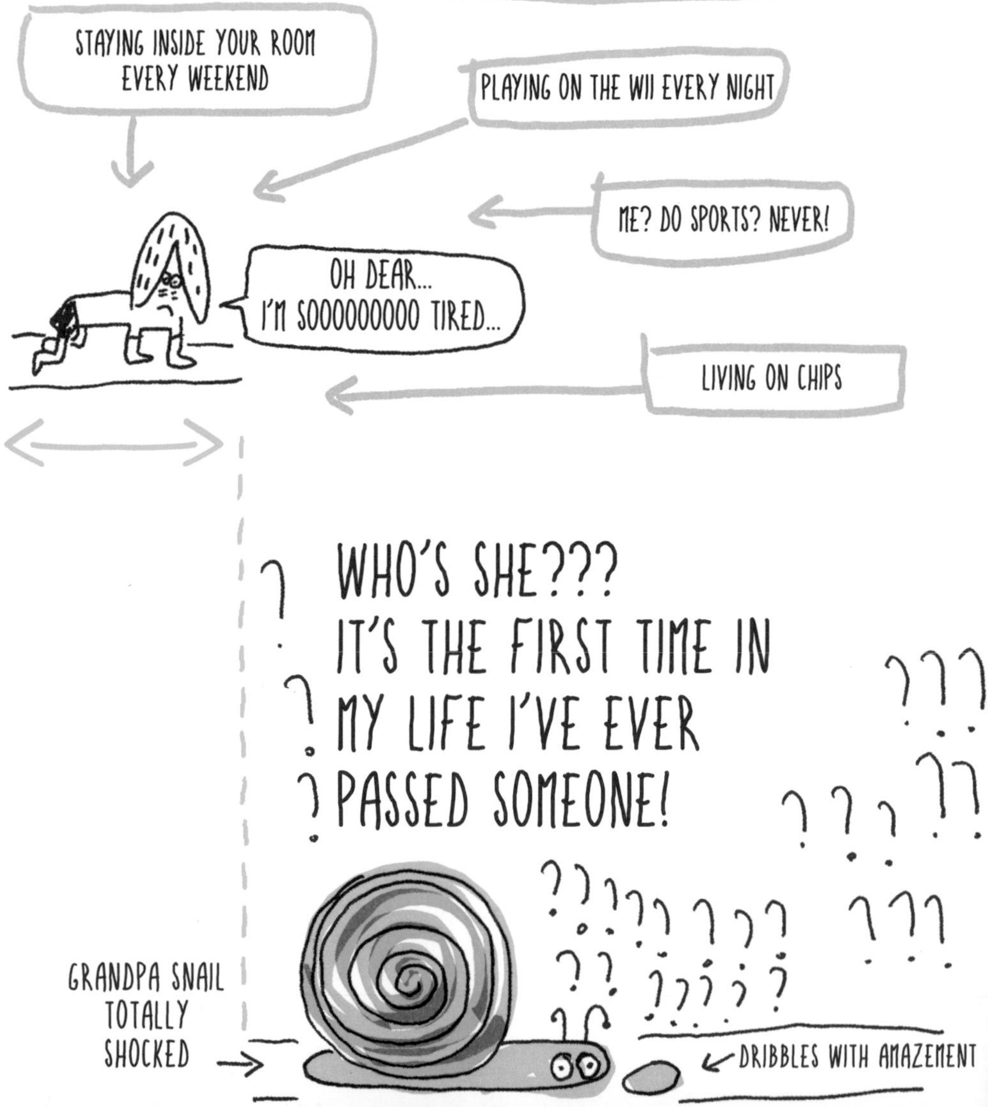

CONTAGIOUS POSITIVE VIBES

BRIGHT-EYED

CAN SPRINT AT 250 MILES PER HOUR

9 HOURS OF SLEEP

TOTALLY RESISTANT TO ALL GERMS

HIGH ACHIEVER!

EATS ARTICHOKES 3 TIMES A DAY

READY FOR ANYTHING!

YUCKY SQUASHED GERM

ARGGH! WHAT NERVE! WHO'S THE BIONIC CREATURE THAT JUST DARED TO PASS ME?

VRRRROOOOOM VROOOOOOOOM

BIG SHOW-OFF IN A FERRARI

USE YOUR ENERGY WISELY. DON'T WASTE IT!

① LIKE THIS:

NOTE: THE AUTHOR WOULD LIKE TO THANK HER CHILDREN FOR PROVIDING THE DIRECT INSPIRATION FOR THIS SCENE

ARGGGGH!!!!!!!
WE'VE RUN OUT OF NUTELLA!!!
THIS IS A NIGHTMARE!!!
WHO'S THE BRAIN-DEAD PERSON
WHO DOES THE SHOPPING
AROUND HERE????

YOUR MOM, TOTALLY EXASPERATED, READY TO ABANDON YOU AT THE LOCAL ANIMAL RESCUE CENTER

YES! I DO HAVE A BRAIN, YOU HORRIBLE, BAD-TEMPERED CHILD! IN FACT, FROM NOW ON DON'T CALL ME "MOM," CALL ME "THE BRAIN." OK?

 **A**

IF YOU FOLLOW THE FANTASTIC ADVICE IN THIS BOOK EVERY DAY:

 **2** FINISH

HOORAY!

WOW! IT'S JUST LIKE BEING AT THE CARNIVAL!

1 START

THE GREAT HAPPINESS SPIRAL

1 START

IT SEEMS UNFAIR, BUT THAT'S LIFE!

BANG

2 FINISH

THE DISASTROUS DOWNHILL SLIDE

WHENEVER YOU GET THE IMPRESSION THAT THE WORLD REALLY IS A BAD PLACE...

 **BEFORE**

BOO HOO!
BOO HOO HOO!
I GOT 5 OUT OF 20 IN ENGLISH...
I'M GOING TO BE BOTTOM OF THE CLASS...
I'M SO DUMB....
MOM AND DAD WILL DISOWN ME...
I'LL HAVE TO RUN AWAY.
LIFE SUCKS!

FLOODS OF DESPERATE TEARS

GET THINGS INTO PERSPECTIVE, MY DEAR...

 **B** — AFTER

> HEY, CALM DOWN!
> I HAVEN'T GOT TUBERCULOSIS.
> I'M NOT DYING OF HUNGER IN AN
> AFRICAN SHANTY TOWN.
> I WASN'T BORN WITH A CONJOINED TWIN SISTER
> (ASK YOUR PARENTS WHAT THIS MEANS).
> I DON'T HAVE TO SLEEP UNDER A BRIDGE.
> I'VE GOT 100,000 FRIENDS ON FACEBOOK AND
> I'M QUITE GOOD-LOOKING. THERE'S MORE TO
> LIFE THAN GRADES!

THERE YOU GO!
EVERYTHING'S FINE AGAIN!

 # ADDED BONUS!

EXCLUSIVELY FOR YOU:
A FREE CONSULTATION WITH MIRMA, THE
GREATEST FORTUNE-TELLER IN THE WORLD

OOOOOOOOOHHHHHHHHH!
DEAREST LITTLE READER,
I SEE A MAAAAAAAARVELOUS,
MAAAAAAGICAL, BRIIIIIIIIIIGHT
FUTURE AHEAD OF YOU!
ALL YOUR DREAMS WILL
COME TRUE!

SO DON'T WORRY,
BE HAPPY!

↑

PERSONAL FORTUNE-TELLER TO THE PRESIDENT
OF THE USA AND HOLLYWOOD SUPERSTARS

AVOID COMPLICATIONS AND DON'T GET DRAWN INTO THINGS

HEY, CAN YOU HIDE THIS HUGE DIAMOND RING AT YOUR PLACE FOR ME? IT'S WORTH $850,000 AND I JUST STOLE IT FROM A JEWELRY STORE

YOU

CHOOSE THE PERFECT ANSWER:

(A) ☐ WITH PLEASURE!

(B) ☐ I'M NOT SURE...

(C) ☐ NO WAY, YOU THIEF

TAKE PITY ON THIS LARGE STARVING FAMILY!!

SCENARIO NO. 1

SCENARIO NO. 2

YOU DON'T GIVE ANYONE A COPY OF THIS BOOK

THANKS TO YOU, THIS BOOK BECOMES AN INTERNATIONAL BESTSELLER

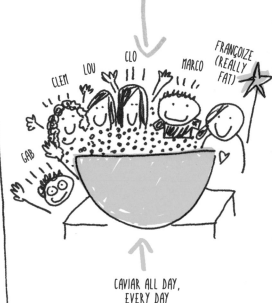

FRANÇOIZE (REALLY FAT)

CLO

LOU

MARCO

CLEM

GAB

CAVIAR ALL DAY, EVERY DAY

GAB

CLEM

LOU

CLO

MARCO

FRANÇOIZE (SKINNY)

6 GRAINS OF RICE

MICROSCOPIC SAUSAGE TO SHARE

THE AUTHOR'S FAMILY

IF, IN SPITE OF ALL THE AMAZING ADVICE IN THIS BOOK, YOU STILL CAN'T FIND HAPPINESS, TALK ABOUT IT. THE WORLD IS FULL OF PEOPLE WHO CAN HELP YOU.

A YOUR PARENTS

SUPER MOM

SUPER DAD

JUST TELL US IF YOU'VE GOT A PROBLEM!

AND WE'LL COME FLYING TO YOUR RESCUE!

ZOOM... ZOOM... ON A MISSION!

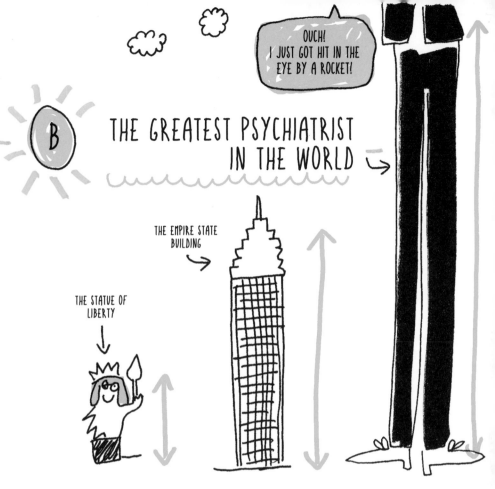

THE GREATEST PSYCHIATRIST IN THE WORLD

B

THE EMPIRE STATE BUILDING

THE STATUE OF LIBERTY

YOUR BEST FRIEND

C

BFF = BEST FRIEND FOREVER

HAPPY ENDING

SEE YOU VERY SOON! FRANÇOIZE

Published in the U.S.A. in July 2014 by Walker Books
for Young Readers, an imprint of Bloomsbury
Publishing, Inc.
www.bloomsbury.com

Bloomsbury books may be purchased for business
or promotional use. For information on bulk
purchases please contact Macmillan Corporate
and Premium Sales Department at
specialmarkets@macmillan.com

Library of Congress Cataloging-in-Publication Data
available upon request • ISBN 978-0-8027-3757-1

Publisher, Nathan: Jean-Christophe Fournier
Design: Albane Rouget
Production: Lucile Davesnes-Germaine
Photogravure: Axiome

Printed in China by Toppan Excel, Guangshou City,
Guangdong

10 9 8 7 6 5 4 3 2 1

AND HERE'S A LIST OF THE OTHER BOOKS I'VE WRITTEN FOR CHILDREN, JUST IN CASE YOU CAN'T LIVE WITHOUT ME! ☺

- HOW COOL* ARE YOUR PARENTS?
*(OR NOT)
- THE BOOK THAT WILL MAKE YOU LOVE BOOKS